Salvatore Calabrese's

Virgin Cocktails

Salvatore Calabrese's

Virgin Cocktails

SALVATORE CALABRESE

PHOTOGRAPHY BY JAMES DUNCAN

STERLING PUBLISHING CO., INC.
New York

TO MY WIFE, SUE. Thanks, again!

Created by Lynn P. Bryan, The BookMaker, London
Designer: Jill Plank
Photography: James Duncan

Library of Congress Cataloging-in-Publication Data

Virgin Cocktails / Salvatore Calabrese.
p. cm.
Includes index.
ISBN 1-4027-1247-2
1. Non-alcholic cocktails. I. Title.
TX814.C27 2004
641.8'75--dc22   2003063336

10 9 8 7 6 5 4 3 2 1

Published by Sterling Publishing Co., Inc.
387 Park Avenue South, New York, N.Y. 10016
©2004 Salvatore Calabrese
Distributed in Canada by Sterling Publishing
C/o Canadian Manda Group, One Atlantic Avenue
Suite 105, Toronto, Ontario, Canada M6K 3E7
Distributed in Great Britain by Chrysalis Books Group PLC
The Chrysalis Building, Bramley Road, London W10 6SP England
Distributed in Australia by Capricorn Link (Australia) Pty. Ltd
P.O. Box 704, Windsor, NSW 2756, Australia

Sterling ISBN 1-4027-1247-2

Contents

Introduction

This is my favorite fantasy. There I am, taking a leisurely break on a Virgin Island set in a clear blue ocean; I am dreaming under a palm tree, which is laden with coconuts. My mouth becomes drier and drier. Oh, for a Coconut Affair. Waiter! Bring crushed ice and a shaker!

In this summer reverie, an exotic woman is walking along the pure white sandy beach, toward me. She has a pale pink flower in her long, dark hair. The sun is shining at its hottest, and the sky has turned an enticing blue. There's not a cloud to spoil the view. I am in Paradise.

Now, what do I really want to drink? Anything with alcohol will spoil the moment. My head will be spinning in moments after the heat and the spirit have combined. Which means no alcohol if I am to remain in this fantasy.

When the challenge to create a new drink presents itself, there have been moments when I discover I have used exotic fruit juices without the addition of alcohol. The inspiration for this book came from one of those moments.

The ultimate virgin cocktail is one untouched by alcohol and the human hand. A cocktail shaken to perfection, and balanced in all flavors. The cocktail's texture is smooth on the tongue, and its aroma piquant; its color reflects the innocent purity of the ingredients.

In practical terms, what makes a virgin cocktail? Fresh fruits, ice (cubed or crushed), just-pressed juices, and an excellent recipe. The garnish and the glass are important, too. Present it with panache and you'll fool most people into thinking it is an exotic cocktail.

Some classic virgin cocktails have remained favorites over the decades, such as the innocent Shirley Temple (sipped on the ubiquitous television program, *Sex and the City*). In her era, the child actress Shirley Temple personified the sweet, well-behaved virginal child with a smile to engage even the most hardened adult.

Plus, there's the weird-sounding Prairie Oyster, the nonalcoholic "cure" for a hangover. (Ever seen an oyster out of its depth, roaming the prairie? Not me!) And spare a thought for the Virgin Mary, a nonalcoholic version of the Bloody Mary—the same tomato red color but no hit of alcoholic vodka!

In the first section, we look at the essential tools and equipment you need to make good virgin cocktails.

They're not that different from the tools you need to make drinks with alcohol. Bartenders apply the same professional criteria to virgins as we do to alcoholics! Also in this section is some information about flavor, about preparing fruit and vegetables for juicing and blending, and about garnishes. However, you'll be pleased to know the rest of the book contains all the best virgin recipes around.

A final note: The measurements are given in both ounces and centiliters. For the purposes of simple conversion, 1oz is equal to 3cl, and so on.

Enjoy!

Salvatore Calabrese

Essentials

Main glass types and sizes

CHAMPAGNE FLUTE	5oz/15cl
COCKTAIL	4oz/12cl
HIGHBALL	10oz/30cl
LIQUEUR	2oz to 3oz/6cl to 9cl
OLD-FASHIONED	5oz to 6oz/15cl to18cl
SHOT	2oz to 3oz/6cl to 9cl
WINE	4oz to 9oz/12cl to 27cl

Liquid essentials

Mixers
club soda
cola
ginger ale
mineral water (still
   and sparkling)
tonic water
7Up

Syrups
gomme syrup
grenadine
Orgeat (almond)
vanilla syrup

Juices
cranberry
lime
lemon
mango
orange
pineapple
tomato
white and pink
   grapefruit

Extras
coconut cream
egg white
fresh gingerroot
ground black pepper
heavy (double)
   cream
salt
superfine (caster)
   sugar
Tabasco sauce
Worcestershire
   sauce

A citrus juicer, a shaker, and a blender are essential tools, as are a small sharp knife, a strawberry huller, and a barspoon.

Ice

Ice must be fresh and dry. Use the best filtered water to make ice or, if you prefer, use bottled spring water. Ice should only taste of water. Ice is used in a blender, a shaker, a mixing glass, or directly in a glass. Why do you need ice? Ice is used to cool juices as they are poured into a glass. Ice is available crushed, shaved, cracked, or cubed. The difference is that cracked and shaved ice are more watery than dry ice cubes. When added to a drink, the juice is immediately diluted. With solid ice cubes, the ice holds its water for longer through the sipping. The average ice cube contains between 1 to 1½ozs (3 to 5cl) water, but the water is released very slowly.

The recipes in this book use hard ice cubes and crushed ice. As a general rule, ice cubes are used for cocktails made in a shaker.

Crushed ice is used for drinks created in a blender. The crushed ice is only used in the blender, not the glass, unless the recipe specifically says to use crushed ice. Ice cubes are used in old-fashioned glasses and highballs, and never in cocktail glasses, unless you are using ice to chill the glass before pouring in the drink.

Many top-quality refrigerators make both ice cubes and crushed ice. If you do not own one of these luxury items, crush your own using a rolling pin. Or buy an ice-crusher. Some ice-cube trays produce fun shapes, such as stars, triangles, and hearts. These add an interesting visual to cocktails.

Also, do not use the ice remaining in a shaker for the next drink, because the ice will be broken and will retain the flavor of the previous drink mixed in the shaker.

An ice scoop is a useful tool, as is an ice-crusher (at the back). A glass
ice-bucket adds a stylish touch to any bar.

Using a shaker

As a general rule, you shake any recipe that contains juice or cream. The most common shakers available today are the Boston shaker (used by many professionals), and the two-piece metal shaker you can buy from any quality home store.

The Boston

The Boston shaker is made of two pieces—one is metal, the other is clear glass. The ingredients are poured in the glass section so you can see what you are doing, then ice is added. The metal part covers the glass, and is gently sealed with a slap of the palm. You will notice it nearly always sits at a sideways angle: this is normal.

Turn the shaker upside down. When the drink is shaken, the liquid will end up in the metal part. Let the drink settle for a moment before parting the two sections. If you can't open it easily, place your thumb under the middle section, where the metal and glass meet, and push gently. This will break the vacuum inside. To serve the drink, pour it through a bar strainer, holding it firmly over the shaker's opening.

The Regular

This consists of a base, a small section with a fitted strainer, and a lid. It's usually compact, small, and easy to handle. Always be sure to hold the lid down firmly. If you get carried away, and it gets stuck, ease the lid up with both thumbs. Sometimes a quick, hard twist will also do the trick. If you have shaken it for a while, wipe the outside with a cloth to warm the sides slightly and loosen the vacuum.

Using a mixing glass

Cocktails whose ingredients mix easily and must be served chilled are made (built) directly into a mixing glass, then poured into a cocktail glass. Always place about six ice cubes into the glass first and, using a barspoon, stir the ice around to chill the glass. Strain off any excess water. Add each juice and stir the mixture well. Strain into a glass.

How to muddle

This is a simple action requiring a little strength in the wrist. To muddle, that is, to mash the fruit in the bottom of the glass, you need a muddler. Sometimes, the end of a barspoon has a muddler as part of its design.

More bartenders are using this method now—instead of bashing the fruits to a pulp, as with a blender.

Muddling brings out the essence and the freshness, and most of the fruit remains intact.

Fruits or mint are muddled directly in the bottom of the glass. Choose a glass with a heavy base. Dice the fruit and place it in the glass or shaker. Add sugar (if stated) and/or a dash of mineral water (if stated) and muddle the fruit.

Juicing

The taste of fresh fruit or vegetables straight from the juicer is a taste to be savored. Luscious, mouth-watering flavors and colors appeal to all of your senses: taste, smell, and sight.

When you walk into a fruit market, the stalls covered with fresh apples, lemons, oranges, and pears are a delight to see and touch. Who can resist picking up an apple and smelling its freshness!

When you unpack the fruit or vegetables at home in the kitchen, treat them with care. If a piece of fruit or a vegetable is packed in plastic, take it out of the packaging. Wash and dry it on paper towels before placing it in the refrigerator. (In summer, it's important to keep fruit chilled.)

When you are considering which recipe to use, think about the flavors you enjoy. Do you like just one juice, for instance, apple? Or orange? Or, you can combine one fruit with another fruit, and a vegetable with another vegetable. Cucumber, ginger, celery, and carrot flavors are tasty when combined and served over ice. However, you can combine vegetables and fruit, too. Look through the recipes and see which ones entice your palate.

Choose your juicer carefully. Whichever design you select, you are going to have to clean it, so it is best to resign yourself to that aspect. Select one that has more than one speed and comes apart easily for cleaning. Be sure to buy one that really does extract the juice from the fruit or vegetable.

Blenders, best for making smoothies and for blending cocktails made with crushed ice, are also a good investment. These are also easier to clean than most juicers.

Place ice and fruit in a blender to make a smooth and chilled mixture.

Preparing fruit for juicing and blending

Wash and pat dry all fruit with skins. Fragile berries such as raspberries, blueberries, blackberries, red and black currants, and cranberries (should you prefer making your own juice as opposed to using ready-made) can be washed, too, in a sieve and left to dry on absorbent paper towels.

Apples Peel, core, and cut in half. Great for juicing.

Pears Peel, core, and dice. Great for juicing.

Bananas Peel and slice in two. Great for blending.

Melons Slice off both ends of a cantaloupe and place it on end on the cutting board. Slice from top to bottom, then remove the rind. Cut in half. Remove the seeds. Dice the juicy flesh. Great for juicing.

Red and white grapes Choose seedless grapes for juicing. Wash and drain on paper towels. Great for juicing.

Crisp apples make delicious juice.

Citrus fruits are an essential sharp ingredient in any cocktail.

Grapefruits, lemons, limes, and oranges Peel, then cut into small segments. Great for juicing.

Kiwi fruit This brown, egg-shaped fruit must be peeled. Dice the green flesh. Great for blending.

Mangoes Peel, then cut the fleshy fruit away from the central seed pod. Great for blending. (Can be messy!)

Strawberries Remove the hull with a sharp bar knife or a handy huller. Dice. Great for blending.

Peaches Peel, cut in half, and remove the stone. Dice the flesh. Great for blending and making purée.

Papayas Cut in half and remove the seeds with a teaspoon (see illustration). Peel and dice the flesh. Great for blending.

Passion fruit Cut in half and scoop out the pulp. Great for blending and using as a garnish on top of the cocktail.

Pineapples Slice off the top and bottom. Place on end on the cutting board and make a cut from top to bottom, removing all of the outer skin. Cut into halves and cut away the hard center core. Great for juicing and blending because it has a fine texture.

Scoop the pips out before you scoop out the flesh.

Flavor

When making a cocktail, it is important to balance the flavors in the recipe. There are four flavors: sweet, sharp (sour), spicy, and bitter. The perfect cocktail is the result of a harmony of one or more, or all four, flavors. Before you choose which cocktail to make, think about what you want from the drink. Each of us has taste buds that are satisfied by different flavors.

Sweetness in cocktails usually comes from sweet juices such as mango, and from the addition of a syrup or sugar.

Sharpness is a flavor that causes you to smack your lips after a sip. Sharpness refreshes your taste buds more than other flavors. Any recipe made with fresh lime or lemon juice will taste sharp, as will a recipe containing raspberries, which have a distinctly sharp taste.

Spicy cocktails are those with a hint of cinnamon or nutmeg, or other such spices.

Bitterness is found in cocktails containing an ingredient made of herbal extracts.

Experiment with flavors

Consider which drinks you immediately like and make a note of the ingredients. Until you have mixed the recipe as given in this book, you will not know exactly how the drink should taste, so make it precisely the first few times, and then experiment. If you prefer a slightly tart taste, add more lemon or lime juice.

Experiment until it is perfect for you. However, if you are making the cocktail for friends, ask them how they prefer it, and tailor the cocktail to please their palates.

Fresh seasonal berries are brilliant for cocktails and smoothies. Here, raspberries, black currants, blueberries, and red currants are ready for the blender.

Garnishes

The garnish is the finishing touch. For a bartender, it can be his visual signature, like the icing on a cake. In virgin cocktails, the garnish is as essential as the mixture in the glass itself. I am particular about the type of garnish I use with a cocktail. It ought to be of a similar color, and must add to a cocktail's flavor. For instance, if you have a citrus-flavored drink, you would not add a slice of peach as a garnish because the flavors would clash. A slim wedge or a thin slice of lemon or orange would be the best choice.

The contemporary style of a garnish is not to overburden the edge of the glass with a foolish fantasy of colorful umbrellas, cherries, and floppy celery stalks. (Although we have seen discreet colored paper umbrellas attempting to make a comeback attempt in a few island bars.) These days, a garnish can also be dropped into the drink. It is a matter of individual style. My favorites are berries, slices or wedges of citrus fruit, and the Cape gooseberry, with its fine outer layers unfurled to reveal the sweet orange fruit inside.

Best places for a garnish

- on the rim of the glass
- on top of the drink
- hanging off the rim, trailing down
- two or three berries on a cocktail stick across the glass
- slice, wedge, or spiral in the drink
- solo maraschino cherry in the drink
- maraschino cherry with a slice in the drink

Citrus garnishes, including spiral, slice, and wedge shapes.

Stirrers, or swizzle sticks, are a great talking point, as well as a fun addition to a virgin cocktail. If you are having a theme party, use stirrers with the same theme: for instance, a Hawaiian lunch calls for swizzle sticks with a pineapple shape on one end. If you're doing a beach party, use shell shapes, or bright blue stirrers.

They are more than just a decorative addition. Some cocktails need to be stirred halfway through the drinking to get the best of the flavors from any berries or fruits on the bottom of the glass.

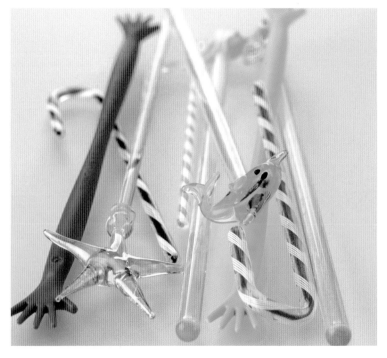

Above: Decorative stirrers can add style to a drink.
Right: Add garnishes such as passion-fruit pulp using a long-handled spoon.
Do this carefully for the best effect.

The recipes

Usually, nonalcoholic drinks are sipped from highballs or tumblers. Some of these recipes are served in cocktail glasses, adding to a sense of the cocktail hour. This means you, the one who prefers not to touch alcohol, can look sophisticated at any party event. Who's to know there's no vodka in the Virgin Oyster Shot in your hand?

The aim of this section is to reactivate an interest in fruit juices and stimulate your palate, and to encourage you to experiment with some exotic juices. These recipes are not designed to be healthy (although they might be); they are a selection of tried-and-tested cocktails that will appeal at different times of the day.

There are many quality juices available in the supermarket, so take advantage of them. However, I always use freshly squeezed orange, lemon, and lime juices. If you make the effort to squeeze your own, you'll see and taste the benefits.

And, when you pick up a supermarket bottle or a carton, check that the ingredients are consistent with the criteria you apply to anything that goes inside your temple (the body). Flavor will be guaranteed.

Key to glass symbols

1   2   3   4   5   6   7   8   9   10   11

1 Cocktail 2 Champagne flute 3 Champagne coupe 4 Highball
5 Old-fashioned 6 Shot 7 Wine 8 Tumbler 9 Goblet 10 Parfait
11 Heat-proof glass

The mouth-watering icy flavor of watermelon dominates in this cocktail.

Acapulco Gold

4oz/12cl	pineapple juice
3oz/9cl	grapefruit juice
1oz/3cl	coconut milk
garnish	slice of pineapple

Shake ingredients sharply with ice. Strain into a tumbler filled with cracked ice. Add the garnish and serve with a straw.

Allegria

The name means "happiness" in Italian. This drink is refreshing, and it has only 78 calories.

1 ripe	small mango, peeled, cut, and diced
1⅔oz/5cl	carrot juice
1⅔oz/5cl	pineapple juice
1⅔oz/5cl	fresh orange juice
⅔oz/2cl	fresh lemon juice
	still mineral water
garnish	a slice of orange and a maraschino cherry

Put the mango pieces in the blender, add the other ingredients, except water, a scoop of ice cubes, and blend. Using the lid to stop the ice from tumbling into the glass, pour the mixture into a goblet filled with fresh ice. Fill to three-quarters. Add the water to dilute the mixture a little. Stir. Garnish with a slice of orange and a maraschino cherry. Serve with a straw.

Acapulco Gold

Apple and Cinnamon Warmer

Makes 10

4 pints/2 liters	**unsweetened apple juice**
3oz/9cl	**fresh lemon juice**
4 tablespoons	**clear honey**
1 large knob	**gingerroot, peeled and sliced**
2	**cinnamon sticks**
6	**star anise**
12	**cloves**
garnish	**small piece of cinnamon stick and an apple wedge**

Place the spices, including the ginger, in a piece of muslin and tie it up. Place in a saucepan and add the apple and lemon juices and the honey. Warm gently, without boiling, for about half an hour. Remove from the heat and take out the bag of spices. Serve in a heat-proof glass. Add the garnish and serve.

Apple and Orange Delight

4oz/12cl	**apple juice**
2oz/6cl	**fresh orange juice**
1oz/3cl	**Rose's lime cordial**
garnish	**slice of apple and a slice of orange**

Add all the juices to a highball filled with ice. Stir well. Add the garnish. Serve with a straw.

Apple-Beet Beauty

2oz/6cl	**apple juice**
2oz/6cl	**fresh beet juice**

Shake the juices with ice and strain into a cocktail glass.

Apple of My Eye

4oz/12cl	**clear apple juice**
½oz/1.5cl	**black currant syrup**
2oz/6cl	**fresh pear juice**
garnish	**apple fan**

Shake all ingredients with ice. Strain into an old-fashioned glass filled with ice. Add the garnish on the rim.

Banana and Strawberry Smoothie

1 large	**ripe banana**
3 tablespoons	**plain natural yogurt**
6	**fresh strawberries**

Peel the banana and break it into pieces. Wash and hull the strawberries and slice them in half. Put everything in the blender. Blend until smooth. Serve in a highball with ice.

Berry Beauty

4oz/12cl	**blueberry juice**
4oz/12cl	**raspberry juice**
1 teaspoon	**clear honey**

Combine all ingredients in a mixing glass with ice. Stir well. Strain into a highball filled with crushed ice. Serve with a straw.

Berry Nice

Blueberries are full of vitamin A and potassium, as are the pears. And the orange juice gives you the vitamin C.

1 cup	**blueberries, fresh or frozen**
1 cup	**black currants**
1	**pear, diced**
1	**orange, juiced**

Wash the fruit. Squeeze the orange juice. Add to the blender with fruit. Blend at medium speed for two minutes. Serve in a tumbler with ice.

Apple of My Eye

Bitter Experience

4oz/12cl	**fresh orange juice**
1oz/3cl	**fresh lime juice**
	bitter lemon
garnish	**lime wedge**

Pour the juices into a highball filled with cracked ice. Top up with the bitter lemon. Stir. Serve with a straw and a stirrer.

Black Sparkle

Serves 2

4oz/12cl	**black currant juice**
4oz/12cl	**fresh orange juice**
4oz/12cl	**apple juice**
	7Up
garnish	**a few black currants and a small sprig of fresh mint**

Pour the juices into a shaker with ice. Shake sharply. Strain into two highballs filled with ice. Top up with 7Up. Stir. Serve with a straw. Garnish by dropping the black currants on top of the drink, and add a sprig of mint into the middle of the drink.

Blueberry Beauty

Serves 2

1 cup	**blueberries**
1	**banana, sliced**
½ cup	**cashew nuts**
1oz/3cl	**light (single) cream**
1 teaspoon	**vanilla essence**
4oz/12cl	**milk**
1 tablespoon	**superfine (caster) sugar**
garnish	**2 fresh blueberries**

Blend all ingredients until smooth. Pour into two tumblers filled with ice. Garnish with two blueberries on a cocktail stick. Serve with a straw.

Bora Bora

4oz/12cl	**pineapple juice**
1oz/3cl	**fresh lime juice**
	dry ginger ale
dash	**grenadine**

Shake all ingredients, except ginger ale. Strain into a highball filled with ice. Top up with ginger ale. Stir. Add the garnish on top of the drink. Serve with a straw.

Cantaloupe Caper

To make the cantaloupe cup
Cut a small slice off the bottom to prevent the cantaloupe from falling over. Cut the top off and cut into a zigzag pattern. Scoop out the seeds and leave about 1/2inch/1.5cm of the fruit.

1 small	**cantaloupe, flesh diced**
3	**strawberries, sliced**
2	**teaspoons clear honey**
2oz/6cl	**plain yogurt**
garnish	**grated nutmeg**

Blend all ingredients, except the nutmeg, until smooth. Add a scoop of crushed ice and blend again for a few seconds. Pour into the cantaloupe cup or a goblet. Serve with a straw.

Carrot and Cranberry Cocktail

A nutritious cocktail that's easy to make and very refreshing.

4oz/12cl	**carrot juice**
2oz/6cl	**cranberry juice**
2 teaspoons	**clear honey**

Shake all ingredients with ice to let ingredients combine well. Strain into a highball filled with ice.

Bora Bora

Casanova's Virgin

The night is still young and he's facing his last, young challenge . . .

1oz/3cl	**raspberry purée**
1oz/3cl	**clear apple juice**
	nonalcoholic sparkling wine
garnish	**3 raspberries**

Shake the purée and the juice with ice. Strain into a chilled champagne flute. Top up with sparkling wine. Stir. Add the three raspberries on a cocktail stick across the glass.

Champ Bleu

Serves 6

1 bottle	**nonalcoholic sparkling wine**
dash	**blue food coloring**

Fill 6 small champagne flutes with the wine and add a drop of blue coloring to achieve the desired depth of blue.

Casanova's Virgin

Cherry Babe

4oz/12cl	**fresh orange juice**
4oz/12cl	**pink grapefruit juice**
1 teaspoon	**fresh lemon juice**
½oz/1.5cl	**juice from maraschino cherries**

In a mixing glass, combine the orange, grapefruit, and lemon juices.
Stir well. Pour into a highball filled with ice. Add the maraschino cherry
juice slowly and watch it settle on the bottom of the glass to create a
two-tone drink.

Cleanser

Serves 4

half	**yellow melon**
half	**papaya**
half	**mango**
6	**strawberries**
½ pint/¼ liter	**passion fruit juice**
½ pint/¼ liter	**peach juice**
1oz/3cl	**grenadine**
juice	**1 lemon**
juice	**1 orange**

Peel the fruit and dice. Place all ingredients in a blender with ice.
Blend until smooth. Strain into a jug and leave until you need it. Serve
in a tumbler filled with ice. If you want to make it less bulky, add a
dash of still mineral water.

Coconut Affair

2oz/6cl	**coconut milk**
3oz/9cl	**fresh orange juice**
3oz/9cl	**pineapple juice**
6	**fresh strawberries, diced**

Blend all ingredients until smooth. Add a scoop of crushed ice and blend again. Pour into a champagne coupe.

Coconut Cooler

Serves 4

6oz/18cl	**coconut milk**
3oz/9cl	**milk**
2oz/6cl	**half-and-half**
flesh	**1 medium coconut**
2oz/6cl	**sugar syrup**
garnish	**wedge of coconut**

Blend all ingredients until smooth. Add two scoops of crushed ice. Blend again for a few seconds. Strain into four tumblers filled with crushed ice. Garnish with a coconut wedge. Serve with a straw.

Coconut Grove

If I had been at the famous nightclub during Frank Sinatra's reign,
I would have created this cocktail for him and his entourage.

3oz/9cl	**pineapple juice**
1⅔oz/5cl	**coconut cream**
1⅔oz/5cl	**fresh pink grapefruit juice**
garnish	**segment of grapefruit and a spiral of orange**

Place ingredients into a blender with a scoop of crushed ice. Blend for
10 seconds and pour into a tumbler. Garnish with a thin segment of
grapefruit and the spiral. Serve with a straw.

Coconut Sublime

3oz/9cl	**fresh orange juice**
3oz/9cl	**pineapple juice**
1oz/3cl	**coconut milk**
garnish	**strawberry**

Blend all ingredients with ice. Strain into a chilled champagne flute.
Garnish with a strawberry on the rim.

Coconut Affair

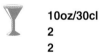
Coffee Digestif

Serves 4

	10oz/30cl	**hot strong black coffee**
	2	**sticks cinnamon**
	2	**tablespoons superfine (caster) sugar**
	garnish	**cinnamon stick, whipped cream, and a dusting of mixed spices**

Add the cinnamon sticks and sugar to the hot coffee. Stir. Allow to cool. Pour over ice cubes into chilled cocktail glasses. Add the garnish.

Cracker

So-called because it is a cracker! It's very simple to make and delicious to sip.

	1⅔oz/5cl	**cranberry juice**
	1⅔oz/5cl	**pineapple juice**
	1⅔oz/5cl	**passion-fruit juice**
	1⅔oz/5cl	**grapefruit juice**
		7Up
	garnish	**slice of lime**

Fill a highball with ice. Add the pineapple, passion fruit, and cranberry juices. Then, add the grapefruit juice. Top up with 7Up. Stir. Garnish with a slice of lime. Serve with a straw and a stirrer.

Cranberry Fruit Cocktail

Serves 2

3oz/9cl	**cranberry juice**
6oz/18cl	**fresh orange juice**
1 cup	**plain yogurt**
1 cup	**sliced peaches**
garnish	**slice of peach and a stem of red currants**

Blend all ingredients until smooth. Add a scoop of ice. Blend again for a few seconds. Strain into two tumblers filled with ice. Add the garnish on the rim. Serve with a straw.

Cranpina

An interesting combination of tart berries with sweet pineapple juice and two citrus fruit juices that makes a refreshing cocktail.

2oz/6cl	**cranberry juice**
2oz/6cl	**pink grapefruit juice**
2oz/6cl	**pineapple juice**
1oz/3cl	**fresh orange juice**

Fill a highball with ice cubes. Pour the first three ingredients into the glass. Stir. Add the orange juice—it will sink slowly down the glass as you drink it, but will look amazing when you first serve the cocktail.

Cranpine Cocktail

Serves 4
An ideal drink for both Thanksgiving and Christmas dinners.

4oz/12cl	**pink grapefruit juice**
4oz/12cl	**pineapple juice**
4oz/12cl	**cranberry juice**
6oz/18cl	**still water**
2oz/6cl	**fresh lemon juice**
	ginger ale
garnish	**a few red currants and a small segment of grapefruit**

In a pitcher, combine the fruit juices and the water. Stir well. Chill for an hour or two. Pour into four highballs filled with ice until three-quarters filled. Top up with ginger ale. Add the red currants and the grapefruit segments on top of the drink. Serve with a straw.

Cucumber Cooler

Deliciously healthy and gives your digestion a helping hand.

4oz/12cl	**apple juice**
quarter	**cucumber, diced**
large sprig	**fresh mint**
garnish	**mint leaves and a cucumber slice**

Blend the cucumber, mint, and apple juice until smooth. Add a scoop of crushed ice. Blend again for a few seconds. Pour into a tumbler. Add the garnish. Serve with a straw.

Cucumber Cooler

Dark Soul

1oz/3cl	**fresh lemon juice**
large handful	**fresh blackberries**
dash	**blackberry syrup**
	7Up
garnish	**three blackberries and a mint leaf**

Shake all ingredients, except the 7Up, with ice. Shake sharply to break down the berries and release the flavor. Pour into an old-fashioned glass. Top up with 7Up. Add the garnish, on a cocktail stick, across the top of the glass.

Elderflower Blend

6oz/18cl	**cranberry-raspberry-elderflower** **tea from a tea bag**
1oz/3cl	**fresh lemon juice**
3	**fresh strawberries**
½oz/1.5cl	**elderflower cordial**
garnish	**1 strawberry in a fan shape**

Make the elderflower tea. Leave it to cool. Place the strawberries in the shaker. Add the lemon juice. Muddle the strawberries lightly. Add the cordial, then the cooled tea. Add ice. Shake sharply. Strain into a highball filled with ice. Add the garnish on the rim. Serve with a straw.

Exotica

Mango, ginger, and orange juices combine to make a sumptuous drink when you need to quench your thirst.

half	**ripe mango, flesh only**
juice	**2 large oranges**
slice	**ginger, peeled and cut into thin strips**
	still mineral water

Slice the mango flesh into the blender, making sure as much loose juice as possible goes in, too. Cut the oranges in half and squeeze on a juice press. Add this to the blender. Add the ginger and some ice cubes. Blend on high for about 30 seconds. Pour into a large highball. Top up with mineral water.

Fiore Cocktail

This drink proves a nonalcoholic cocktail has all the excitement and mystery of one with alcohol! It looks supremely elegant and delicious.

1oz/3cl	**lychee juice**
1oz/3cl	**clear apple juice**
1oz/3cl	**cranberry juice**

Shake all ingredients with ice. Strain into a chilled cocktail glass.

Forest Fizz

Imagine the juices oozing from these berries. That's just a hint of what this drink tastes like.

handful	**fresh blueberries**
handful	**fresh blackberries**
6 to 8	**fresh raspberries**
⅓oz/1cl	**fresh lemon juice**
1 teaspoon	**superfine (caster) sugar**
	club soda
garnish	**selection of berries and a sprig of mint**

Place the berries in a blender with the lemon juice. Sprinkle the sugar over the berries. Blend until smooth. Strain the mixture through a nylon strainer or a fine cheesecloth into a highball filled with ice. Top up with soda. Stir. If you can, use blueberry soda to give this a better flavor. Garnish with a selection of berries on a cocktail stick across the drink, and a sprig of mint on top in the middle. Serve with a straw.

Fresh Fancy

4	**celery stalks, washed and trimmed**
20	**seedless white grapes**
3oz/9cl	**fresh apple juice**

Juice the celery stalks, including the leafy bits. Juice the grapes, and then the apples. Stir. Serve in a tumbler filled with ice.

Fiore Cocktail

Frosty Strawberry Delight

3oz/9cl	**pineapple juice**
1	**egg white**
1	**tablespoon clear honey**
½ cup	**strawberries, diced**
3oz/9cl	**fresh orange juice**
garnish	**small strawberry**

Blend the pineapple juice, egg white, honey, and strawberries for about 10 seconds. Take the lid off and add some orange juice, replace the lid, and blend again. Repeat this action until the orange juice is combined. Pour into chilled champagne flutes. Add a strawberry to the rim of the glass.

Gelub (Rose Water)

Serves 2
This is a classic exotic cocktail taken from the Arabic word from which the renowned "julep" is derived.

6oz/200g	**red/pink rose petals, washed**
3oz/100g	**superfine (caster) sugar**
2 pints/1 liter	**water**
1oz/3cl	**fresh lemon juice**
garnish	**1 rose petal**

Place the petals in a saucepan with the sugar, water, and lemon juice. Simmer for 10 minutes. Take off the heat, and cool. Pour into flutes filled with ice. Add a rose petal on top. Adjust the sweetness to taste.

 Fresh Fancy

Ginger Alert

Here's a nonalcoholic cocktail that is very good for your system as well as being very tasty. Ginger is an ancient remedy used to improve digestion and help the circulation. It's also good for helping to relieve nausea and any inflammation. This delicious cocktail is designed to give your system a wake-up call, and has a subtle fusion of ginger and apple flavors.

3oz/9cl	**clear apple juice**
1⅔oz/5cl	**clear pear juice**
⅔oz/2cl	**fresh lemon juice**
small piece	**fresh gingerroot**
	ginger ale
garnish	**apple wedge**

Pour the apple, pear, and lemon juices into a shaker with ice. Grate the ginger into the shaker. Shake well to infuse the ginger flavor. Strain into a highball with ice. Top up with ginger ale. Stir. Add the garnish. Serve with a straw.

Ginger Zest

All of the exotic flavors of the Orient are in this spicy, fresh, and healthy cocktail.

2⅓oz/7cl	**fresh carrot juice**
2⅓oz/7cl	**tomato juice**
teaspoon	**clear honey**
1oz/3cl	**fresh lemon juice**
2 to 3 slices	**fresh gingerroot**
dash	**Worcestershire sauce**
garnish	**yellow cherry tomato and a basil leaf**

Place the ginger into a shaker. Muddle to release the essence, then pour in all ingredients. Add a scoop of ice cubes. Shake for 10 seconds. Pour into a highball, letting the ice fall into the glass as well. Garnish with a red and a yellow cherry tomato, each cut in half and speared by a cocktail stick, with a basil leaf between them.

Great Grenadian

1oz/3cl	**raspberry purée**
1oz/3cl	**peach purée**
2oz/6cl	**pink grapefruit juice**
2oz/6cl	**passion fruit juice**
few slices	**fresh gingerroot**
1 teaspoon	**clear honey**
garnish	**half a passion fruit**

Place the gingerroot in the shaker and add the honey. Muddle. Add the remaining ingredients. Shake well with ice. Strain into an old-fashioned glass over crushed ice. Add the garnish. Serve with a straw.

Guache Guava

Serves 2

7oz/21cl	guava juice
6oz/18cl	pineapple juice
5	fresh strawberries
1oz/3cl	fresh lime juice
garnish	lime wedge

Blend all ingredients until smooth. Add a scoop of crushed ice. Blend again for a few seconds. Pour into two tumblers. Add the garnish. Serve with a straw.

Hawaiian Virgin

4oz/12cl	pineapple juice
2oz/6cl	coconut cream
dash of	blue food coloring
garnish	pineapple wedge and maraschino cherry

Pour the pineapple juice into a blender. Add the coconut cream and the food coloring. Add crushed ice and blend. Pour into a tumbler. Garnish with a wedge of pineapple and a maraschino cherry. Serve with a straw.

Great Grenadian

Healing Smoothie

This drink protects and heals the stomach lining and is especially useful for making you feel better when you have a hangover.

1	**firm kiwi fruit**
quarter	**cantaloupe, with the skin**
1	**ripe banana**

Push the kiwi and the cantaloupe through a sieve. Place the juice and banana in a blender and blend until smooth. Serve in a tumbler.

Indian Apple

Serves 2

4oz/12cl	**apple juice**
4oz/12cl	**unsweetened Lapsang Souchong tea**
1oz/3cl	**cranberry juice**
	7Up
garnish	**an apple slice and mint leaves**

Pour all ingredients, except for the 7Up, into a large pitcher filled with ice. Add the garnishes. Stir. Add the 7Up. Stir. Serve in a chilled champagne coupe.

Hawaiian Virgin

Island Surfer

The combination of these two colorful fruits and juices produces a smooth-textured drink full of flavor.

3oz/9cl	**fresh mandarin orange juice**
2oz/6cl	**pineapple juice**
1	**kiwi fruit, peeled and diced**
4	**strawberries, diced**
garnish	**slice of kiwi fruit**

Blend all ingredients until smooth. Add a scoop of crushed ice and blend again. Pour into a large goblet. Garnish with a slice of kiwi fruit. Serve with a straw.

Jewel

4oz/12cl	**fresh orange juice**
1oz/3cl	**fresh lime juice**
2 dashes	**raspberry juice or sirop de framboises**
	chilled 7Up

Shake the first two juices with ice. Strain into a chilled champagne flute. Top up with 7Up. Stir. Slowly drop the raspberry juice into the drink. It will become a two-tone color.

Jewel

Kiwi Cooler

Lots of vitamin C and E in this magical drink.
Serves 4

6	**kiwi fruit, peeled and diced**
2oz/6cl	**gomme syrup**
3oz/9cl	**fresh lemon juice**
	still mineral water
garnish	**kiwi fruit wedge**

Blend the kiwi fruit, gomme, and lemon juice until smooth. Add a scoop of crushed ice. Blend again for a few seconds. Fill four tumblers with crushed ice and strain the mixture in, filling about halfway. Top up with still mineral water and stir. Garnish with a kiwi fruit wedge.

Kiwi Punch

Serves 10

12	**kiwi fruit**
1⅔oz/5cl	**kiwi syrup**
2oz/6cl	**fresh lemon juice**
2 bottles	**alcohol-free wine**
1 quart/liter	**7Up or club soda**
garnish	**peeled kiwi fruit and small strawberries**

Peel and blend the kiwi fruit and strain through cheesecloth to collect the juice. Or use an electric juicer; then you will not need to strain the liquid. Add the sugar to the mixing bowl. Stir.

Pour the alcohol-free wine into a punch bowl and mix in the kiwi fruit and sugar mixture. Add the 7Up or soda (this gives a drier taste). Garnish with a few slices of peeled kiwi fruit and small strawberries afloat in the punch. Serve in wine glasses.

Lanesborough Cooler

1oz/3cl	**Orgeat (almond syrup)**
⅔oz/2cl	**fresh lemon juice**
1oz/3cl	**fresh lime juice**
	7Up
garnish	**lime wedge**

Fill a goblet with ice cubes. Add the syrup and juices. Top up with 7Up. Garnish with a lime wedge dropped in the glass.

Lean Machine

Serves 2

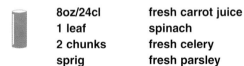

8oz/24cl	**fresh carrot juice**
1 leaf	**spinach**
2 chunks	**fresh celery**
sprig	**fresh parsley**

Blend all ingredients until smooth. Strain the mixture into two highball glasses filled with ice.

Lemonade

Serves 2

Multiply the ingredients by the number of people for whom you want to make this cooling drink.

1	**lemon**
2 tablespoons	**superfine (caster) sugar**
cup	**boiling water**
2oz/6cl	**fresh lemon juice**
cup	**ice water**
garnish	**lemon slices**

Remove the zest from the lemon. Add it to a measuring cup with the sugar and boiling water. Stir well to dissolve the sugar. Leave to cool. When cool, take out the lemon zest and add the ice water, then the lemon juice. Stir well. Pour into two highballs filled with ice cubes. Add a lemon slice into the drink, and one on the edge of the glass.

Lemonade

Lilac Beauty

If you can't find fresh berries, use frozen, and thaw them beforehand.

2 tablespoons	**low-fat plain yogurt**
2oz/6cl	**white grape juice**
handful	**fresh blueberries**
handful	**fresh blackberries**
garnish	**2 berries**

Combine all ingredients in a blender until smooth. Strain into a goblet. Garnish with two berries on top of the drink. Serve with a straw.

Lime Life-Saver

Makes 2 small glasses
Great for the morning after, when you need to build up zest. The ginger stimulates your system, and the addition of vitamins from the carrots make this an essential restorative cocktail.

2	**fresh limes**
6	**medium carrots**
fair-sized	**knob gingerroot**
2	**apples**

Cut the limes in half and juice. Juice the carrots. Peel the ginger and juice it. Cut the apples and juice them. Stir and pour equally into two small tumblers.

Limey

Serves 10

10oz/30cl	**fresh lime juice**
10oz/30cl	**fresh lemon juice**
3 pints/1.5 liters	**sparkling mineral water**
6 large dashes	**Angostura bitters**
2 tablespoons	**superfine (caster) sugar**
garnish	**slices of lemon and lime.**

Place the sugar in a large bowl and add the juices and bitters. Stir until the sugar has dissolved. Add ice. Add the sparkling water just before guests arrive. Stir. Add the garnish in the wine glass.

Luscious

This is a healthy cocktail, tasting crisp and appetizing.
Serves 2

2	**fresh apples**
2	**fresh pears**
1	**fresh orange**

Peel and slice the fruit and place in the juicer. Stir. Serve immediately in two old-fashioned glasses filled with ice.

Lynn's Wonder

4oz/12cl	**apple juice**
quarter	**cucumber, diced**
sprig	**fresh mint**
garnish	**mint leaves and a cucumber slice**

Blend all ingredients until smooth. Add a scoop of crushed ice. Blend again for a few seconds. Pour into a tumbler. Add the garnish. Serve with a straw.

Magic Moment

You really want to catch the moment these ingredients come together for a full burst of flavor. It's very simple to make. And very easy to drink more than one...

3oz/9cl	**red or white grape juice**
⅔oz/2cl	**fresh lemon juice**
⅔oz/2cl	**strawberry syrup**
	club soda
garnish	**a few grapes**

Pour the juices and syrup into a highball filled with ice. Top up with soda. Stir. Garnish with a few grapes sitting on the rim of the glass. Serve with a straw.

Luscious

Mango Cocktail

Mangoes are high in beta-carotene and a good source of vitamins E, A, and C. This is a great health-reviving drink.
Makes 1 large drink

half	**ripe mango**
juice 1	**orange**
juice 1	**lime**
large handful	**fresh raspberries**

Take the seed out of the mango and scoop out the flesh. Cut the citrus fruit in half and juice them. Put it all in the blender with a few ice cubes. Blend until the mixture is smooth. Pour into a large tumbler.

Mangococo Cocktail

Serves 4

1 large	**mango, peeled and diced**
6 large	**wrinkled passion fruit**
7oz/21cl	**coconut milk**
6oz/18cl	**passion-fruit juice**
garnish	**mango wedge**

Scoop out the passion-fruit flesh. Blend all ingredients with a few ice cubes until smooth. Strain into four highball glasses filled with ice. Add the garnish and serve with a straw.

Mangococo Cocktail

Mango Frappé

Serves 2

A frappé is a partially frozen drink made with lots of fruit and frozen until small ice crystals form on top.

half	mango, peeled and sliced
4	kiwi fruit, peeled and diced
half	banana, sliced
4	strawberries, sliced
1	tablespoon clear honey
¼ cup (65ml)	plain yogurt
garnish	sprinkle freshly grated nutmeg

Place all ingredients (except the nutmeg) in a blender and blend until thick and smooth. Pour into a shallow dish suitable for placing in the freezer. Freeze until crystals form on the top. Take out of the freezer and spoon into cocktail glasses. Add a sprinkle of freshly grated nutmeg as a final touch. Serve with a straw and a small spoon.

Melon Treat

4oz/12cl	watermelon juice
4oz/12cl	cantaloupe juice
1 tablespoon	mango purée
garnish	wedges of cantaloupe, watermelon, or orange

Juice the melons, purée the mango flesh, and measure the required amount. Combine the ingredients in a tall parfait glass. Garnish with a wedge of each fruit on a cocktail stick, placed into the glass.

Mint Sparkler

Serves 6

1 bottle	**sparkling nonalcoholic white wine**
10oz/30cl	**apple juice**
2oz/6cl	**fresh lime juice**
sprig	**fresh mint leaves**
garnish	**spiral of lemon**

Place all liquid ingredients into a punch bowl with ice. Stir. Add the mint leaves, taking them off the stem as you go. Serve in wine glasses. Add the garnish on the rim.

Mocha Mad

4oz/12cl	**milk**
1 tablespoon	**instant chocolate powder**
1 tablespoon	**instant coffee**
1 large scoop	**ice cream**

Blend all ingredients with crushed ice until smooth. Pour into a highball. Serve with a straw.

Moonlight

Serves 2

half	**banana, sliced**
4oz/12cl	**fresh orange juice**
4oz/12cl	**grapefruit juice**
4oz/12cl	**pineapple juice**
2oz/6cl	**white cranberry juice**
garnish	**strawberry and a mint leaf**

Pour all ingredients into a blender with crushed ice. Blend until smooth. Pour into two goblets. Place the mint into the top of the strawberry, make a slice in the bottom of it, and place it on the side of the glass.

My Fair Lady

Serves 2

6oz/18cl	**raspberry juice**
6oz/18cl	**white grape juice**
6oz/18cl	**pink grapefruit juice**
3oz/9cl	**fresh lemon juice**
dash	**gomme syrup**
garnish	**a few grapes, sliced, and raspberries**

In a large pitcher filled with ice, mix all the juices. Strain into two highballs filled with ice. Garnish with the slices of the grapes and the whole raspberries dropped in the drink. Stir. Serve with a straw.

Moonlight

My Mint Tea

Serves 2
My wife, Sue, likes to drink this sitting in the garden room on a hot afternoon. This is a very good digestif, and soothing to the stomach.

bunch	**fresh mint**
1 quart/liter	**boiling water**
1oz/3cl	**fresh lemon juice**
1 teaspoon	**lavender honey**
garnish	**fresh lime slice and mint sprig**

Put the mint leaves in a heat-proof pitcher and pour the boiling water over them. Add the honey and lemon juice. Stir to infuse the ingredients. Leave to cool naturally. When cool, remove the mint leaves. Pour the liquid into two highballs filled with ice. Add a sprig of fresh mint and a slice of lime.

Neat Beet

Beetroot is a powerful cleanser and a great source of vitamin B-6. Combines well with carrots and citrus fruits.
Serves 2

2	**large carrots**
1	**small beetroot**
2	**oranges (preferably blood oranges)**

Scrub carrots and beetroot. Cut off stems, and slice into pieces. Cut the oranges in half and squeeze them. Pour the juice equally into two tumblers. Juice the beet and carrots and add this mixture to the orange juice already in the glasses. Stir and drink quickly.

On the Beach

Where else do you want to go on a sultry summer's day? Once there, this will quench your thirst.

1	**ripe yellow melon, diced**
handful	**raspberries**
3⅓oz/10cl	**fresh orange juice**
⅓oz/1cl	**fresh lime juice**
dash	**grenadine**
	7Up
garnish	**melon balls and raspberries**

Blend all ingredients for 10 seconds without ice, then add a scoop of ice. Blend again. Pour into a goblet filled with ice. Top up with 7Up. Stir. Garnish with melon balls and raspberries spiked on a cocktail stick laid across the glass. Serve with a straw.

Orange Blossom Special

3oz/9cl	**fresh orange juice**
2oz/6cl	**mandarin juice**
half	**banana**
1 teaspoon	**clear honey**
garnish	**mandarin segment**

Blend all ingredients until smooth. Pour into a tumbler filled with ice. Add the garnish on the edge of the glass, and serve with a straw.

Papa's Papaya

This is one of my favorite fresh juice cocktails to wake your body's system up in the morning. It's full of vitamins.
Makes 2 large drinks

1	**papaya**
1	**small ripe banana**
6	**mandarins**

Peel the papaya, scoop out and discard the seeds. Chop the flesh roughly and place in the blender. Peel the banana, break into chunks, and add to the blender. Cut mandarins in half and juice them. Add juice to the blender. Add a few ice cubes. Blend everything until smooth. Serve in large tumblers.

Papa's Papaya

On the Beach

Passion Fruit and Mango Cooler

Both of these exotic fruits are mouth-wateringly delicious, their flesh hidden under tough exteriors. Once you cut through the skins, you will see texture and smell their fruity fragrances. The mango is slightly messy to deal with, so have kitchen towels handy.
Serves 4

1	**fresh mango**
8	**passion fruit**
2oz/6cl	**gomme syrup**
3oz/9cl	**fresh lime juice**
	still mineral water
garnish	**pulp from half a passion fruit**

Peel and dice the mango. Scoop out the pulp from the passion fruit. Place the mango flesh and passion-fruit pulp into a blender. Add the lime juice and the gomme syrup. Blend until smooth. Add a scoop of ice, and blend again for a few seconds. Fill four highballs with crushed ice and strain in the mixture to halfway. Top up with mineral water. (Add less water if you want it to be thicker.) Stir. Add the garnish on top of the drink. Serve with a straw.

Peach Passion

Serves 2

1	**fresh peach, skinned and sliced**
6oz/18cl	**apricot juice**
6oz/18cl	**fresh orange juice**
6oz/18cl	**fat-free milk**
1 teaspoon	**clear honey**
garnish	**grated nutmeg, slice of peach**

Blend all ingredients, except the nutmeg, until smooth. Add a scoop of crushed ice and blend again for a few seconds. Pour into a goblet. Add the sprinkling of nutmeg, and a slice of peach on the edge of the glass. Serve with a straw.

Peachy Raspberry Delight

This is sweet and full of flavor. The peaches are full of vitamin A, vitamin C and beta-carotene. Brilliant to make in the red currant season.
Serves 2

3	**ripe peaches**
handful	**raspberries**
handful	**berries from sprigs of red currants**

Halve the peach, pull out the stone, and slice the peach flesh into a blender. Add the berries, and a splash of still water to help the blending process. Blend until smooth. Pour into two small tumblers filled with ice.

Piña Copaya

Papaya juice is rich in vitamins A and C, and its nutritional highlight is its useful enzymes. And it has a wonderful flavor.

small wedge	**peeled pineapple**
half	**papaya, peeled and pitted**
⅔ cup	**fresh coconut, grated**
½oz/1.5cl	**still water**

Juice the pineapple and papaya. Blend the juice, coconut, and water on high until smooth. Strain the pulp. Serve in a tumbler.

Pineapple Crush

A delicious cocktail with an intriguing texture and a great combination of sweet and sour flavors.

1	**large slice of pineapple**
1oz/3cl	**fresh lemon juice**
4	**passion fruit**
	sugar to taste

Cut a slice of pineapple and remove the rind. Cut it into chunks and juice them. Add the lemon juice, stir, and pour the mixture into a pitcher. Stir in the pulp from three passion fruit. Add sugar to taste (depending on how sharp the pineapple tastes). Fill a small tumbler with the mixture, and top with the pulp from the remaining passion fruit.

Pineapple Crush

Pink Palace

4oz/12cl	**pineapple juice**
4oz/12cl	**grapefruit juice**
4	**strawberries, sliced**
half	**small banana, sliced**
garnish	**small strawberries**

Blend all ingredients until smooth. Pour into a white wine glass. Thread two small strawberries on a cocktail stick and add to the glass.

Pink Velveteen

4oz/12cl	**guava juice**
1oz/3cl	**fresh lemon juice**
1 teaspoon	**clear honey**
3	**fresh ripe figs**
garnish	**fig wedge**

Skin the figs, slice them, and place in a small bowl. Add the honey and the lemon juice. Muddle the mixture until it is a consistent, smooth paste. Add the mixture into a shaker with ice. Add the guava juice. Shake sharply. Strain into an old-fashioned glass filled with crushed ice. Add the garnish on the rim. Serve with a short straw.

Pink Velveteen

Prairie Hen

This is one of those cocktails to take the morning after the night before! It's not that pleasant to taste, unless you like bitter drinks.

2 dashes	**vinegar**
2 barspoons	**Worcestershire sauce**
1	**free-range egg (don't break the yolk!)**
2 dashes	**Tabasco sauce**
	salt and pepper to taste

Pour all ingredients into a small wine glass. Down in one gulp.

Prairie Oyster

This is a piquant pick-me-up for the morning after the night before.

1 teaspoon	**virgin olive oil**
1 tablespoon	**tomato ketchup**
dash	**Worcestershire sauce**
1	**free-range egg yolk**
dash	**white-wine vinegar**
	salt and pepper to taste

Rinse a wine glass with the olive oil and discard the oil. Add the tomato ketchup and the egg yolk. Season with the Worcestershire sauce, wine vinegar, and salt and pepper. Close your eyes and drink in one gulp. Serve a small glass of iced water on the side.

Pussyfoot

A pleasant fruit drink, enriched by egg yolk, for those who like to drive home after a party.

5oz/15cl	**fresh orange juice**
1oz/3cl	**fresh lemon juice**
1oz/3cl	**fresh lime juice**
	free-range egg yolk
1 to 2 dashes	**grenadine**
garnish	**maraschino cherry and orange slice**

Shake all ingredients with ice. Strain into a highball filled with ice. Garnish with a slice of orange and a maraschino cherry on a cocktail stick.

Raspberry Blusher

3oz/9cl	**raspberry juice**
3oz/9cl	**grape juice**
1oz/3cl	**fresh lemon juice**
¼ teaspoon	**almond extract**
	ginger ale
garnish	**sprig of mint and 1 raspberry**

In a mixing glass, stir all the juices and the almond extract. Then place in the refrigerator to chill. Just before serving, add ice to a highball, and then top up with ginger ale. Add the garnish on a cocktail stick. Serve with a straw.

Raspberry Lassi

Serves 4

2 cups	**fresh raspberries**
10oz/30cl	**natural yogurt**
3 teaspoons	**clear honey**
3 tablespoons	**rosewater**
garnish	**rose petals**

Blend all ingredients with a few ice cubes until smooth. Strain into four small tumblers filled with ice. Drop a few rose petals in the drink and add one rose petal on top. Serve with a straw.

Raspberry and Orange Smoothie

A delicious deep raspberry color, this is as smooth as anything.
Serves 2

5 handfuls	**raspberries**
4oz/12cl	**fresh orange juice**
8oz/24cl	**fresh natural yogurt**
10 to 12	**mint leaves**

Rinse the berries and add them to a blender. Add orange juice, yogurt, and mint leaves. Blend until smooth. Serve in a tumbler filled with ice.

Raspberry Mint Cooler

handful	**fresh raspberries**
sprig	**fresh mint leaves**
	ginger ale
garnish	**3 raspberries and a mint leaf**

Place the raspberries and the mint into a blender with two scoops of crushed ice. Blend until smooth. Pour into a goblet. Add ginger ale and stir. Garnish with three raspberries on a toothpick and a mint leaf.

Red Apple Fizz

Crisp apples make the best juice; combine their flavor with sweetness and bubbles, and you have a tempting fizz.

1oz/3cl	**fresh apple juice**
dash	**passion fruit syrup**
dash	**grenadine**
	ginger beer

Pour the juice, passion fruit syrup, and grenadine into a highball filled with ice. Stir. Top up with ginger beer. Stir. Serve with a stirrer.

Sangrita

Serves 10

This is a traditional Mexican drink that wakes up your taste buds.
Prepare at least two hours before you plan to serve it at a party.

35oz/100cl	**tomato juice**
16oz/48cl	**fresh orange juice**
5 teaspoons	**clear honey**
3oz/9cl	**fresh lime juice**
pinch	**salt**
1	**chili, finely chopped**
½ teaspoon	**white onion, finely chopped**
	ground black pepper
10 drops	**Worcestershire sauce**

Pour all ingredients into a mixing bowl. Stir well. Place in the
refrigerator to chill for about two hours. Then, strain into a large glass
pitcher. Serve in wine glasses.

Sensation

This perfect combination of sharp, sweet, and spicy flavors creates a taste sensation.

3oz/9cl	**tomato juice**
1⅔oz/5cl	**passion fruit juice**
1⅔oz/5cl	**carrot juice**
⅓oz/1cl	**fresh lemon juice**
1 teaspoon	**clear honey**
4 dashes	**Worcestershire sauce**
garnish	**cherry tomato and a sprig of basil**

Pour all ingredients into a shaker filled with ice. Shake well to dissolve honey. Pour the mixture into a highball filled with ice. Garnish with a cherry tomato and a sprig of basil.

Sharp Starter

Serves 6

1 bottle	**nonalcoholic white wine**
6oz/18cl	**ginger beer**
3oz/9cl	**tonic water**
pinch	**ground ginger**
pinch	**cayenne pepper**
garnish	**few sliced grapes and a twist of lemon**

Pour all ingredients into a large pitcher and stir. Add ice cubes to chill the liquid. Add the garnish to the pitcher. Serve in six wine glasses.

Sensation

Shirley Temple

A classic from the 1960s, this is a favorite nonalcoholic "cocktail" that tempts even the most jaded palate.

	ginger ale
2 to 3 dashes	**grenadine**

Pour the ginger ale into a highball filled with ice. Add the grenadine. Stir. Serve with a stirrer.

Singapore Swing

4oz/12cl	**fresh orange juice**
4oz/12cl	**pineapple juice**
half	**small banana, sliced**
4	**strawberries**
1 tablespoon	**clear honey**
garnish	**strawberry and a slice of orange**

Blend all ingredients until smooth. Pour over ice into a highball. Add the garnish on a cocktail stick. Serve with a stirrer.

Slim Jim

4oz/12cl	**pink grapefruit juice**
4oz/12cl	**tomato juice**
2 to 3 dashes	**Worcestershire sauce**
garnish	**celery stick and lime wedge**

Shake all ingredients with ice. Strain into a highball filled with ice. Add the garnish.

Sportsman

1oz/3cl	**lime cordial**
1oz/3cl	**fresh lemon juice**
1 teaspoon	**rose hip syrup**
	tonic water
garnish	**lemon and lime slices**

Pour ingredients, except for tonic water, into a goblet with ice. Add the tonic water and stir. Add the garnish.

St. Clement's

4oz/12cl   **fresh orange juice**
4oz/12cl   **bitter lemon**
garnish   **orange slice**

Pour the orange juice, then the bitter lemon, into a highball filled with ice. Stir, and add the garnish.

Star Anise Cocktail

Serves 6

12 to 14   **star anise**
8oz/225g   **stem ginger in syrup**
4 pints/2 liters   **sparkling mineral water**

Using still mineral water, freeze the star anise in ice cube trays overnight. Blend the stem ginger and its syrup with a little mineral water for about a minute. Pour a large teaspoon of the mixture into each highball. Add the star anise ice cubes to each glass. Then top up with sparkling water. Stir. Serve with a stirrer.

Star Anise Cocktail

Strawberry Field

6	**fresh strawberries**
handful	**raspberries**
6oz/18cl	**fresh orange juice**
1oz/3cl	**fresh heavy cream**
sprig	**mint**
garnish	**strawberry and a mint leaf**

Blend all ingredients until smooth. Add a scoop of crushed ice. Blend again. Pour into a large wine glass. Add the garnish on the rim of the glass. Serve with a straw.

Strawberry Passion

Serves 4
Serve this drink chilled, when it will taste even more fruity and delicious. It has a great combination of flavors.

1lb/450g	**fresh strawberries**
4 large	**wrinkly passion fruit**
10oz/30cl	**fresh orange juice**
grated zest	**1 orange**

Dice the berries and place them in a glass bowl. Cut the passion fruit in half, take out the flesh and seeds with a teaspoon, and add to the strawberries. Stir in the orange juice and the zest. Chill for an hour or so before serving in tumblers.

Summer Sunset

Serves 4

A refreshing cocktail full of vitamins and energy—the papaya contains medicinal qualities—to take you through the day, whatever you may be doing.

half	**yellow melon**
half	**papaya**
half	**mango**
6	**strawberries**
7oz/20cl	**passion-fruit juice**
7oz/20cl	**peach juice**
1	**lemon, cut in half**
1oz/3cl	**fresh orange juice**
3 dashes	**grenadine**
garnish	**small sprig of mint, strawberry**

Scoop out the seeds from the fruit and discard. Dice the fruit. Put it into a blender and add the passion-fruit and peach juices. Add a squeeze of lemon and the grenadine. Blend for 10 seconds. Add two scoops of ice cubes and blend again to chill the drink. (If preparing a day in advance, do not add ice until ready to serve.) Fill four highballs with ice and fill each three-quarters full. The drink will be pale red.

The final touch: using a barspoon, float the fresh orange juice over the top. It will sit on top of the juices, and gradually drizzle its way in fine strands to the bottom of the glass. Garnish with a small sprig of fresh mint set in the top of a strawberry. Serve with a straw.

Sun Grove

6oz/18cl	**fresh orange juice**
1oz/3cl	**fresh lime juice**
few slices	**fresh ginger**
	club soda
garnish	**slice of orange and a maraschino cherry**

Place the ginger in a shaker and lightly muddle it to release the flavor. Add the orange and lime juices. Add some ice. Shake well. Strain into a highball filled with ice. Top up with soda. Stir. Add the garnish. Serve with a straw.

Note: If you prefer it sweeter, use 7Up instead of club soda.

Sunset

2 teaspoons	**pomegranate juice**
	ginger ale
garnish	**maraschino cherry**

Fill a white wine glass, filled with ice, three-quarters full with ginger ale. Add the pomegranate juice. Drop the garnish in the drink.

TJ Cocktail

2oz/6cl	**apple juice**
1oz/3cl	**fresh orange juice**
sprig	**fresh mint**
2 slices	**fresh gingerroot**

Shake all ingredients with ice for quite a while to let the ice break down the gingerroot and the mint leaves. Strain into a chilled cocktail glass.

Temptation

Serves 2

4	**pear halves (canned)**
6oz/18cl	**pear juice**
4oz/12cl	**fat-free milk**
half	**banana, sliced**
2 scoops	**vanilla ice cream**
garnish	**pear wedge**

Blend all ingredients until smooth. Add a scoop of crushed ice and blend again for a few seconds. Pour into two goblets. Add the garnish. Serve with a straw.

Tomato-Cucumber Cocktail

Serves 2

8oz/24cl	**tomato juice**
1 cup	**cucumber, diced**
2 teaspoons	**onion, chopped**
1oz/3cl	**fresh lemon juice**
2 dashes	**hot pepper sauce**
garnish	**lime wedge**

Blend all ingredients until smooth. Pour into a highball glass and add the garnish.

Trio Brillo

Serves 2

This is a cleansing cocktail, and is full of vitamin C and fiber.

22	**blackberries**
22	**raspberries**
4	**handfuls red currants**
	7Up
garnish	**blackberry and raspberry on a cocktail stick**

Rinse the berries and place into a blender. Blend until smooth. Pour into a highball filled with ice. Top up with 7Up. Stir. Add the garnish.

Tomato-Cucumber Cocktail

Tropic

4oz/12cl	**mango juice**
2oz/6cl	**blood orange juice**
½oz/1.5cl	**fresh lemon juice**
teaspoon	**superfine (caster) sugar**
	sparkling mineral water
garnish	**mango wedge and half a slice of orange**

Shake all ingredients, except for the mineral water, with ice. Strain into
a highball filled with ice. Top up with mineral water and stir. Add the
garnish.

Tropicana

All the exotic tastes of the tropics are combined in this creamy cocktail
that's perfect on a summer's day.

1oz/3cl	**coconut milk**
2oz/6cl	**pineapple juice**
2oz/6cl	**mango juice**
1	**small banana, peeled and diced**
garnish	**Cape gooseberry**

Blend all ingredients for a few seconds. Add a scoop of crushed ice.
Blend again. Pour into a goblet. Garnish with a Cape gooseberry set
on the rim. Serve with a straw.

Trio Brillo

Ugly Virgin

3oz/9cl	**mandarin juice**
3oz/9cl	**pink grapefruit juice**
	7Up
garnish	**grapefruit wedge**

Add the mandarin juice, followed by the grapefruit juice, into a highball filled with ice. Add the 7Up. Stir. Add the garnish.

Up-Beet

12oz/36cl	**tomato juice**
12oz/36cl	**beetroot juice**
	salt and black pepper
dash	**Worcestershire sauce**
dash	**fresh lemon juice**

Pour the two juices over ice in a mixing pitcher. Add a squeeze of lemon juice, salt, pepper, and Worcestershire sauce. Stir. Strain into a cocktail glass.

Virgin Bellini

2oz/6cl	**peach purée**
	nonalcoholic sparkling wine
garnish	**peach wedge (optional)**

Add the peach puree into a chilled champagne flute. Top up with the nonalcoholic wine. Stir. Add the garnish if desired.

Virgin Bullshot

It is said that if you don't want to start lunch with soup, then start with a Bullshot. It's invigorating, with a hint of lemon flavor.

5oz/15cl	**beef bouillon**
dash	**fresh lemon juice**
2 dashes	**Worcestershire sauce**
pinch	**celery salt**
dash	**Tabasco sauce**
	ground black pepper
garnish	**lime wedge**

Shake the bouillon, lemon juice, Tabasco, and Worcestershire sauces in a shaker. Strain into a highball. Add a quick twist of black pepper. Garnish with a lime wedge on the rim. Serve with a stirrer.

Virgin Caesar

5oz/15cl	**clamato juice**
⅔oz/2cl	**fresh lemon juice**
pinch	**celery salt**
dash	**Tabasco sauce**
2 dashes	**Worcestershire sauce**
	black pepper
garnish	**lime wedge**

Pour the clamato and lemon juices over ice into a highball glass. Add the spices and stir. Add a quick twist of black pepper. Garnish with a lime wedge on the edge of the glass.

Virgin Caipirinha

A Brazilian name for the most popular cocktail, usually made with cachaça. This gives you the flavors without the distracting alcohol kick!

half	**lime, diced**
half	**small lemon, diced**
half	**small orange, diced**
1	**sugar cube**
	ginger beer
garnish	**sprig of mint**

Place the fruit in the bottom of a mixing glass. Add the sugar cube and a dash of ginger beer. Muddle. Strain into an old-fashioned glass filled with crushed ice. Top up with ginger beer. Add the garnish on top of the drink. Serve with a straw.

Virgin Caipirinha

Virgin Colada

This is a commonly requested coconut-flavored cocktail. It's a Piña Colada without the rum!

4oz/12cl	**pineapple juice**	
2oz/6cl	**coconut cream**	
garnish	**pineapple wedge and a maraschino cherry**	

Pour the pineapple juice into a blender. Add the coconut cream. Blend for a few seconds. Add the crushed ice and blend again. Pour into a colada glass or a tumbler. Garnish with a wedge of pineapple and a maraschino cherry. Serve with a straw.

Virgin Cosmopolitan

For people in a party mood—who don't want sex in the city.

3oz/9cl	**cranberry juice**
½oz/1.5cl	**orange cordial**
½oz/1.5cl	**Rose's lime cordial**
½oz/1.5cl	**fresh lime juice**
garnish	**orange spiral**

Shake all ingredients with ice. Strain into a chilled cocktail glass. Add the garnish.

Virgin Cosmopolitan

Virgin Eggnog

This is an eggnog without the brandy! Here's an amusing tale: A regular came into the bar at Christmas and asked for an eggnog; however, I had to make it without the brandy because he was taking antibiotics, and without the egg because he had high cholesterol. So, I mixed this for him, and handed it him, saying, "Here's your milk, sir."

6oz/18cl	milk
1	free-range egg yolk
sprinkle	cinnamon powder
1 teaspoon	caster sugar
garnish	freshly grated nutmeg

Shake all ingredients with ice. Strain into a wine glass. Add a sprinkle of nutmeg over the drink.

Virgin Fizz

2oz/6cl	fresh orange juice
	nonalcoholic sparkling white wine
garnish	half a slice of orange

Pour the chilled orange juice into a chilled champagne flute. Top up with the sparkling wine. Stir gently. Add the garnish.

Virgin Fruit Fusion

1oz/3cl	**kiwi-fruit purée**
½oz/1.5cl	**kiwi-fruit syrup**
½oz/1.5cl	**elderflower cordial**
6oz/18cl	**fresh grapefruit juice**
garnish	**slice of kiwi fruit**

Shake all ingredients with ice. Strain into a highball filled with ice. Add the garnish and serve with a straw.

Virgin Lea

An award-winning cocktail that's a perfect combination of sweet, spicy, and sharp flavors in one sip.

4oz/12cl	**tomato juice**
1⅔oz/5cl	**passion-fruit juice**
half	**yellow bell pepper, sliced**
1 teaspoon	**clear honey**
1 to 2 dashes	**Worcestershire sauce**
garnish	**cherry tomatoes and a basil leaf**

Place the pepper slices in a blender and add the juices. Blend for 10 seconds at low speed. Add honey, Worcestershire sauce, and ice cubes. Blend at high speed for 10 seconds. Pour through a strainer into a highball filled with ice. Garnish with a cherry tomato and a sprig of basil on a cocktail stick. Sit a cherry tomato on the rim. Serve with a straw and a stirrer.

Virgin Madras

6oz/18cl	**cranberry juice**
2oz/6cl	**fresh orange juice**
garnish	**lime wedge**

Pour all ingredients into a highball filled with ice. Stir. Garnish with a lime wedge.

Virgin Mary

A delicious spicy pick-me-up you can drink as a tonic when you feel the need for one.

5oz/15cl	**tomato juice**
1oz/3cl	**fresh lemon juice**
1 to 2 dashes	**Worcestershire sauce**
	salt and ground black pepper
1 to 2 dashes	**Tabasco sauce**
	celery stick

Pour the tomato juice into a highball filled with ice. Season to taste with the spices. Stir well. Add the celery stick to use as a stirrer.

TJ Cocktail

Virgin Fizz

Virgin Cocktails

Virgin Mojito

1 teaspoon	**superfine (caster) sugar**
⅔oz/2cl	**fresh lime juice**
bunch	**fresh mint on the stem**
	sparkling water

Put the sugar and lime juice in the bottom of a highball with a thick base. Add the mint leaves and muddle with the end of a barspoon or a wooden muddler. This releases the essence from the mint. Fill the glass with crushed ice. Top up with sparkling water. Stir. Serve with a stirrer.

Virgin Oyster Shooter

1	**fresh virgin oyster**
2oz/6cl	**clamato juice**
1 slice	**cucumber, diced into small pieces**
½oz/1.5cl	**fresh lemon juice**
dash	**Tabasco sauce**
dash	**Worcestershire sauce**
pinch	**salt**
	black pepper

Place the oyster into a shot glass. Shake the remaining ingredients with ice. Strain into the shot glass. Drink in one gulp, letting the oyster slide down your throat.

Virgin Madras

Virgin Raspberry Daiquiri

2oz/6cl	**raspberry purée**
1oz/3cl	**pineapple juice**
½oz/1.5cl	**fresh lime juice**
2 dashes	**raspberry syrup**
garnish	**3 perfect raspberries**

Shake all ingredients with ice. Strain into a chilled cocktail glass.
Place the three raspberries on a cocktail stick across the glass.

Virgin Sea Breeze

3oz/9cl	**cranberry juice**
2oz/6cl	**fresh grapefruit juice**
garnish	**lime wedge**

Pour the ingredients into a highball filled with ice. Stir. Add the
garnish. Serve with a stirrer.

Virgin Oyster Shooter

Virgin Sour

One green apple can help make the day healthy. Combine it with the succulence of strawberries and bananas, and it's perfect!

6	**fresh strawberries**
1	**green apple**
1	**banana**
	still mineral water
garnish	**apple fan**

Peel and core the apple and juice it. Dice the strawberries. Peel the banana. Place all ingredients into a blender with a scoop of crushed ice. Blend until smooth. Pour into a highball glass. Add a dash of mineral water and stir. Add the garnish.

Watermelon Frappé

Makes 10

1	**small watermelon, seeded and diced**
5 tablespoons	**superfine (caster) sugar**
2 cups	**crushed ice**

Place a quarter of the crushed ice into a blender. Add a quarter of the melon flesh and the sugar and blend until smooth. Pour the mixture into a pitcher and put to one side. Repeat the process three times to make up the right amount. Pour into 10 tumblers.

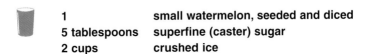

Watermelon Frappé

Index

Acknowledgments

I would like to thank everyone involved in putting this book
together, especially Sterling Publishing for having such faith in
me to do another cocktail book.
To Fiona Lindsay, to Lynn Bryan, and to James, a big thanks
to you all for your work.
To Stevan Relic and Giancarlo Mancino, thanks for your help.

The BookMaker would like to thank Dartington Glass
and William Yeoward for the loan of stylish glasses to make
the cocktails even more glamorous.
Thanks, Alan, for your help.